GREAT MYSTERIES

ANCIENT MYSTERIES

There are many ancient sites and events, from all over the world, that for centuries have been shrouded in mystery. Explanations have been found for some of these mysteries through the work of archaeologists and scientists, but many remain unexplained. What was the purpose of Stonehenge? Is there any truth in the power of the Mummy's Curse? Why did the Nazca Indians draw huge pictures on the desert floors of Peru? All these questions, and many more, are investigated and discussed in this collection of facts and opinions about some of the world's most famous and puzzling ancient mysteries.

In 1975, a hot-air balloon was flown over the Nazcan lines of Peru in an attempt to prove that the Nazcans used this method to see their strange designs over a thousand years ago.

GREAT MYSTERIES

ANCIENT MYSTERIES

Rupert Matthews

Illustrated by Nik Spender

The Bookwright Press
New York · 1989

Great Mysteries

Ancient Mysteries
Monster Mysteries
Sea Mysteries
UFOs

Cover Illustration: Admiral Roggeveen and his group of Dutch explorers look in awe at the strange statues of Easter Island.

First published in the
United States in 1989 by
The Bookwright Press
387 Park Avenue South
New York, NY 10016

First published in 1988 by
Wayland (Publishers) Limited
61 Western Road, Hove
East Sussex BN3 1JD, England

Library of Congress Cataloging-in-Publication Data

Matthews, Rupert.
    Ancient mysteries/Rupert O. Matthews; [Illustrated by Nik Spender].
       p.   cm. — (Great mysteries)
    Bibliography: p.
    Includes index.
    Summary: Presents unsolved mysteries from the pre-Christian era of the ancient world, including the statues on Easter Island, the mound builders, and the Nazcan Plain.
    ISBN 0-531-18246-0
1. Curiosities and wonders — Juvenile literature. [1. Curiosities and wonders.]
I. Spender, Nik, ill.   II. Title.   III. Series: Great mysteries series.
AG243.M355 1989   88-6899
001.9′4′093 — dc19   CIP
                                                   AC

Phototypeset by Oliver Dawkins Ltd, Burgess Hill, West Sussex RH15 9LH.
Printed in Italy by G. Canale & C.S.p.A., Turin.

Contents

Introduction

The past has always fascinated people. Whether the subject is their own history, or that of their relatives, most people are interested in the events of the recent past. Even more intriguing are the stories from farther back in history. The details of some ancient events are very well known, but others remain mysteries.

The secrets attached to many ancient events have remained hidden because these events date from times before people could write and record their history. This period is known as prehistoric.

Stonehenge, for example, is a magnificent prehistoric monument, which stands on Salisbury Plain in England. There is no mystery about its existence; the huge stones stand there for all to see. However, nobody knows why Stonehenge was built or what its significance might have been. If the people who built Stonehenge had been able to write, they might have recorded the purpose of the monument and how it was used. If they had, the mystery surrounding Stonehenge would not exist.

Without such records, archaeologists have to search for evidence at the monument itself. Using any information they can find, archaeologists have formed many theories to explain how and why Stonehenge was built.

Right *Pieces of pottery, known as shards, help archaeologists to date sites.*

Above *Egyptian writing, known as hieroglyphics, was first translated about 100 years ago. Until then the history of ancient Egypt was unknown.*

There are other ancient mysteries that date from a time when writing was well known and records were kept. Unfortunately, over the centuries many books and manuscripts have been lost or destroyed during wars. Because of this, modern historians sometimes find that they know only some of what happened at a particular time. In order to understand the rest of the story, historians must search for clues in existing books and manuscripts.

Many puzzling events have had more than one explanation suggested for them. In this book, we shall be looking at some of the most famous ancient mysteries and at some of the ideas that have been put forward to solve them.

An imaginary Celtic ceremony

It is dark. The eastern sky has begun to lighten, but no rays of sunshine light the scene. A large group of people dressed in long white robes approach the stones. They walk along the pathway between two earthen banks, which run up the hill from the northeast. Three men lead the group.

The procession reaches the circular bank and passes silently into the sacred enclosure. The three leaders pass between two stones and enter the great circle of upright stones. Most of the people remain outside the stone circle. They strain to see what the three men are doing.

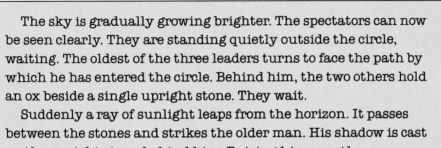

The sky is gradually growing brighter. The spectators can now be seen clearly. They are standing quietly outside the circle, waiting. The oldest of the three leaders turns to face the path by which he has entered the circle. Behind him, the two others hold an ox beside a single upright stone. They wait.

Suddenly a ray of sunlight leaps from the horizon. It passes between the stones and strikes the older man. His shadow is cast on the upright stone behind him. Raising his arms the man chants softly. Then he turns, advances on the ox and kills it. The ox collapses on the ground. Outside the circle, the people sigh with relief. The Sun God has received his sacrifice.

The Standing Stones

The gaunt outline of Stonehenge rises above the slopes of Salisbury Plain in southern England. The vast circle of standing stones lies beside a main road and is easy to find and to visit.

The ruined stone monument is impressive by its size. The tallest stones are 6.7 meters (22 ft) high and weigh about 50 tons. However, the way in which these huge stones are assembled seems little short of amazing.

Archaeologists and historians have been interested in Stonehenge for many years. During the eighteenth century, it was mistakenly believed that Stonehenge had been built by the druids. These priests were Celts who came to Britain from France and Germany about 450BC. The druids sometimes offered humans in bloody ceremonies of sacrifice. It was therefore thought that Stonehenge might have been a temple in which sacrifice was common.

At dawn, the circle of Stonehenge is silhouetted against the rising sun.

But during the twentieth century, fresh excavations at Stonehenge yielded much important information. The first construction on the site now occupied by Stonehenge was the bank and ditch, which can still be seen. This circular earthwork is the "henge" of Stonehenge, constructed about 3200BC. It is thought that within the ditch was built a large, circular wooden building. This may have been used to keep dead bodies. Such buildings are known as charnel houses.

Also erected at this early time was the Heel Stone, which stands outside the circular bank. It is clear that this monument was constructed so that it aligned with the moon. The entrance to the henge faced the most northerly moonrise, which occurs only once every eighteen years. The Heel Stone marked the place on the horizon where the moon would be seen to rise part way through this eighteen-year cycle.

The central circle of Stonehenge is seen here through the main entrance of the henge — a circular bank and ditch that surrounds the stone monument.

11

Right *The largest sarsen stones at Stonehenge form the central trilithons — a group of three stones, as shown here.*

Below *In 1958 government scientists excavated Stonehenge and re-erected some of the fallen stones.*

It seems that after many years of use, the henge and its wooden building were abandoned. It was not until about 2200BC that new building work was carried out.

About eighty boulders of bluestone were brought to the site and erected in a double circle at the center of the henge. The origin of these bluestones is a mystery in itself. The nearest source for this particular type of stone is in the Prescelly Mountains of South Wales, 210 kilometers (130 mi) from Stonehenge.

The new Stonehenge was very different from the old structure. Not only was stone used instead of timber, but it faced the midsummer sunrise. It is thought that a new people may have brought a new religion to the area.

Around Stonehenge

Stonehenge lies at the center of a vast area of prehistoric sites. One of the most mysterious is the Great Cursus. Nobody knows why it is there or what purpose it once served. It is made up of two banks of earth about 1 meter (3 ft) high and 100 meters (330 ft) apart that run for 3 kilometers (2 mi) across Salisbury Plain.

Before the bluestone circles were completed they were demolished. New, larger stones, known as sarsens, were brought to the site from the Marlborough Downs, about 32 kilometers (20 mi) to the north.

Once at Stonehenge, the sarsens were shaped and placed upright in pits dug to hold them. The horizontal stones, known as lintels, were then pulled up, probably on a ramp built on the outside of the sarsens, and placed on top of the upright sarsens.

The most obvious explanation for this monument is that it was a temple. However, it has been found that the locations of many stones are relevant to dozens of different astronomical events. It has therefore been suggested that Stonehenge was a type of astronomical observatory.

Whatever the true purpose of Stonehenge, be it charnel house, observatory, temple or sacrificial altar, it remains one of the most mysterious structures in Britain. For thousands of years, the stones have stood on their windswept site on Salisbury Plain. Let us hope that they remain there for many years to come, until one day their mystery is revealed.

Date Chart

3200BC Stonehenge I, a timber building surrounded by a bank and ditch, is erected. After several centuries it is abandoned.

2200BC About eighty bluestones are brought from Wales and erected to form Stonehenge II.

2000BC Stonehenge II is demolished. Sarsen stones are brought to the site and Stonehenge III is erected.

1500BC The bluestones are returned to Stonehenge and erected within the sarsen circle.

About **1000BC** Stonehenge is abandoned.

Stonehenge is one of the most famous stone monuments in northwest Europe. This structure, also used as a burial chamber, is Kits Coty House in England.

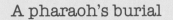

A pharaoh's burial

The hot desert sun blazes down. The sunlight sparkles on gold, silver and glittering jewels. Everywhere there are the signs of extravagant wealth. Yet the only sounds to be heard are the tramp of thousands of feet and continuous wails of mourning.

The people of Egypt are burying the dead pharaoh, their god-king. They have built a mighty pyramid to his memory. Already his mummified body lies in a chamber deep in the center of the huge structure. Now his mourners are placing the pharaoh's belongings, as well as precious gifts, inside the tomb. The people believe that the pharaoh will be able to use these objects in his afterlife, and he must be supplied with the best of everything.

Beautiful clothes are carried into the tomb for the dead pharaoh to wear. The dead god-king's magnificent palace furniture and weapons are laid around his body, so that they will be on hand whenever he should want to use them. Before the tomb is sealed, the priests will lay sacred curses upon the chamber. These are intended to deter any person from stealing the rich treasures from the pharaoh's tomb.

Journey to the Afterlife

Few things are more fascinating than the pyramids of Egypt and the mummies that they were built to conceal. The greatest of the pyramids, and in many ways the most mysterious, are those that stand at Giza in northern Egypt.

Built for the pharaohs of the 4th dynasty, the pyramids of Giza are about 4,500 years old. The largest of all pyramids was built here for the Pharaoh Khufu. The size of the Great Pyramid is stupendous, yet the bulk of the structure is not the only impressive feature. Its measurements are amazingly accurate. The lengths of each side vary by no more than 20 centimeters (8 in). Perhaps even more impressive is the fact that the Great Pyramid is positioned on a line running north to south that varies by no more than 0.08 of a degree. The feat of placing so many huge blocks of stone together so accurately must have called for incredible engineering skills.

The impressive pyramids at Giza are found on the outskirts of Cairo and have become the most recognized collection of ancient Egyptian tombs.

The extraordinary preservation of Egyptian mummies is shown by the head of Pharaoh Rameses II who died more than 3,500 years ago.

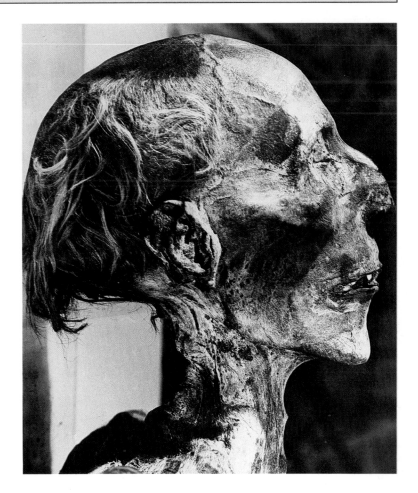

The early pharaohs, including Khufu, were looked upon as gods. Every command of a pharaoh became law. It was believed that when a pharaoh died, his spirit, or *ka*, continued to live. The *ka* would need the luxuries with which the pharaoh had been familiar during life. Most important of all, the *ka* required that the body be preserved as a home for the *ka*. It was this belief that led the Egyptians to mummify the royal bodies and to bury rich objects with their dead kings. In order to protect the pharaohs, priests laid curses on the tombs, threatening death to anyone who should disturb them.

17

Left The wealth buried with the pharaohs was stupendous. Tutankhamen's coffin, shown here, was made of solid gold.

In 1923, the tomb of Pharaoh Tutankhamen was discovered. The find caused a worldwide sensation, for this was the first time that an unplundered tomb had been opened. Inside the tomb an inscription read, "Death will slay with his wings whoever disturbs the peace of the Pharaoh."

Below On one of the photographs of a mummy case from the temple of Amun-Ra, the face of an evil woman is said to have appeared instead of the case.

An ancient Egyptian mummy case, now in the British Museum.

Weeks later Lord Caernarvon, who had financed the expedition, died of a strange fever. Within months thirteen of the twenty men who opened the tomb were dead.

Another tale follows the terrible trail of misfortune that followed a mummy case from the temple of Amun-Ra, a god of ancient Egypt. This mummy case was bought in Egypt by the historian Douglas Murray at the turn of the century. Soon after the purchase, Murray lost his arm in an accident and two of his traveling companions died.

Murray decided to sell the mummy case and had it photographed. On one frame the photographer was said to find, instead of a mummy case, the face of a real woman staring at him with an expression of hatred. A few days later the photographer died. Murray then gave the mummy case to the British Museum. Within a day, one of the two porters who carried the case to the museum broke his leg and the other was killed in a traffic accident. Eventually two exorcists were called in to dispell the spirit. The mummy case caused no further trouble.

The stories associated with the Mummy's Curse may well be based on exaggerations and coincidence. However, the ancient Egyptians who built the pyramids left more than one mystery behind them.

Date Chart

About **2850 BC** Egypt is united under the rule of the first pharaohs.

About **2660 BC** The first pyramid is built for Pharaoh Zoser at Sakkara.

About **2500 BC** The Great Pyramid is built at Giza.

1349 BC Pharaoh Tutankhamen is buried.

341 BC Egypt is conquered by Alexander the Great.

1923 The opening of the tomb of Pharaoh Tutankhamen.

A defeated legion

Most of the Romans are dead. Those still able to stand cluster around the sacred Eagle, standard of the legion. All around are the yelling Picts, the enemy that has reduced a proud legion of fighting troops to a handful of desperate men.

For a moment the barbaric crowd pulls back from the attack. A Pictish chieftain runs out in front of his men. He begins to chant an old battle song. The men begin to sing. Soon hundreds of voices are raised in song.

The remaining Roman legionaries take a firmer grip on their swords and shields. A few of them glance up at their holy standard. They would willingly die rather than allow the Eagle to fall into the hands of the enemy. Grimly, the handful of men turn to face their enemies.

The Picts end their song and with a great cry of triumph, the horde rushes forward. The Romans fight desperately, but it is not long before the last is killed. The Pictish chieftain grabs hold of the Eagle and lifts it into the air. At last, they have conquered this once powerful Roman legion.

The Legion of the Lost

The army of ancient Rome was the most efficient fighting organization of its day. The most important formations of the army were the legions, which consisted of about 6,000 highly trained men. The mystery surrounding the fate of one of these legions, the IX, has puzzled historians for many years.

The IX Legion was one of the oldest legions in the Roman army. The IX Hispana, as they were known, first went to Britain as part of the Roman invasion force in AD43. The legion fought several battles against the British warriors and was ultimately victorious. Then, after a close battle with the British Iceni in AD60, the Romans pushed their frontier farther north, to York.

Here, the IX Legion built a massive fortress surrounded by a protective fortification. The duties of the legion would

This map shows the Roman forts, roads and legionary fortresses in England and Wales at the time of the IX Legion.

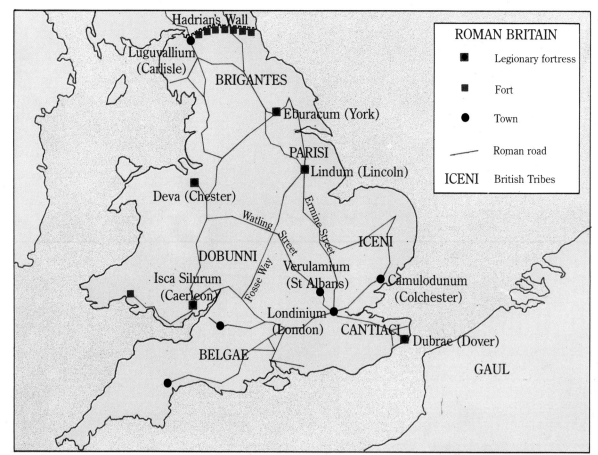

ROMAN BRITAIN
- ■ Legionary fortress
- ■ Fort
- ● Town
- — Roman road
- ICENI British Tribes

Hadrian's Wall
Luguvallium (Carlisle)
BRIGANTES
Eburacum (York)
PARISI
Lindum (Lincoln)
Deva (Chester)
Watling Street
Ermine Street
ICENI
DOBUNNI
Fosse Way
Verulamium (St Albans)
Isca Silurum (Caerleon)
Camulodunum (Colchester)
Londinium (London)
CANTIACI
Dubrae (Dover)
BELGAE
GAUL

A reconstruction of a Roman ballista, used as a weapon that hurled iron darts at the enemy. These weapons may well have been used by the IX Legion.

have consisted chiefly of patrolling the area. The local people, the Brigantes, had only recently been defeated. It was important for Roman soldiers to patrol regularly through Brigantian villages to prevent rebellion.

At the same time, many of the tribes farther north had not been conquered and remained hostile to Rome. These tribes often carried out raids into Roman territory. The IX Legion was expected to fight off any attacks.

For many years the IX Hispana carried out these duties well. However, after AD 108, the legion simply disappears from official Roman documents. It clearly ceased to exist, but no mention is made anywhere of how this came about. The fate of 6,000 highly trained and experienced men is a complete mystery.

The Legions of Varus

If the IX Hispana was wiped out in battle, it would not have been the first legion to suffer this fate. In AD 9 Governor Varus led three Roman legions into Germany in order to conquer fresh territories. However, the army was ambushed by the Germans, and the legions wiped out. Six years later a Roman patrol found the skeletons of the dead legionaries scattered across the floor of a forest.

Many suggestions have been made regarding the disappearance of the IX Hispana. It is known that in AD122 the VI Legion was transferred to Britain. The men of the VI were employed in building the huge defense work known as Hadrian's Wall. When the wall was completed, the VI was stationed at York. Clearly the IX had left by this time.

Some historians have used this fact to suggest a likely fate for the IX. Perhaps the IX Hispana was involved in a terrible defeat in northern Britain. If the whole legion had been wiped out in the battle, it would not have been re-formed. If this were the case, the entire legion would have had to be replaced. The VI Legion might have been brought in for this purpose.

Other historians point to the fact that the IX may have been in existence some years after AD122. The gravestone of one officer of the IX seems to indicate that he served in the Legion closer to AD130. A further piece of evidence comes from building materials that belonged to the IX found in Germany.

Hadrian's Wall, in Northumberland, England, was built by the Romans, soon after the disappearance of the IX Legion.

Left *Archaeological excavations at the Roman fort of Vindolanda, in Northumberland, England. It is through such excavations that historians learn about life in Roman times.*

On this evidence it has been suggested that the IX Hispana was transferred to Germany in AD122 to make way for the VI Legion in York. The IX Legion may then have met their fate fighting the Germans.

A third theory rests on neither set of evidence. During the early second century, when the IX disappeared, rebellions were not uncommon. It is possible that the IX Legion took part in such a rebellion and was defeated. In such circumstances the legion would have been disbanded in disgrace and never re-formed.

It seems, however, that whether these men were defeated in battle, were transferred to another country, or rebelled, we will never know how or why the IX Legion disappeared.

Date Chart

AD43 The IX Legion takes part in the invasion of Britain.

AD60 About 2,000 men of the IX Legion are killed by tribesmen led by Queen Boadicea.

About **AD82** The IX Legion is moved to York, where a large fortress is constructed.

AD108 The final mention of the IX Legion.

AD122 The VI Legion is brought to Britain.

Admiral Roggeveen and the long-eared statues

It is Easter Day 1722. Admiral Roggeveen has landed on an island in the Pacific Ocean on his travels from Holland. No European has ever seen this island before and it is not named on maps or charts. Admiral Roggeveen names it Easter Island, in commemoration of the date of his discovery.

Once ashore, Roggeveen and his men are staggered to find, scattered around the island, dozens of enormous stone statues. The sheer size of the statues is impressive and some of Roggeveen's men become wary of this strange place. There were no statues on any other island the Dutchmen had visited. Roggeveen is fascinated by the statues with their hollow eyes, long earlobes and pointed chins.

He asks an islander about the statues. He tells Roggeveen that they walked to their places during the time of the "Long Ear" rulers. Roggeveen asks who the "Long Ears" were. The islander becomes angry and refuses to answer. Soon afterward, Admiral Roggeveen leaves Easter Island, excited and mystified by his discovery and the origin of these impressive statues. As his ship sails away, he looks back wondering whether he will ever discover how and why these mysterious statues were built.

The Statues of Easter Island

Almost 2,000 kilometers (1,200 mi) from the nearest land, Easter Island covers 120 square kilometers (46 sq mi) and is the site of one of the world's greatest mysteries. On the slopes of the island stand dozens of strange statues. All the figures are alike. Their deep eyesockets have no eyes. Their earlobes are long and their chins pointed. The statues stand silently gazing across the bare landscape. Nobody knows who built these dramatic statues, or why.

Recent scientific research, however, has brought some facts to light. It is now known that the stone figures, of which there are about a thousand, were carved inside the crater of Rano Raraku, an extinct volcano on the island. Scattered around this quarry are many unfinished statues. Some are nearly completed, others barely started. Beside the stone figures lie many stone-working tools. It is as if the workmen put down their tools one evening and never returned.

Mystery surrounds the method by which the islanders transported the statues and set them up. Some of the stone figures lie 16 kilometers (10 mi) from the quarry. Dragging a weight of up to 30 tons across the broken countryside

Right Many of the statues, such as these shown here, were overturned and damaged by islanders after a rebellion against the "Long Ears." These have been re-erected in recent years.

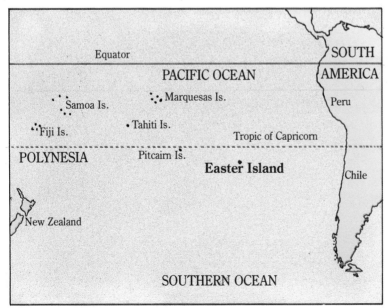

Left A map showing the position of Easter Island in the Pacific Ocean.

of Easter Island would have been a tremendous task. Nobody is sure how the feat was managed without heavy ropes or large wooden rollers. Setting the stone men upright on their bases would have been even more difficult.

Left *The blank stares and long earlobes of the Easter Island statues make them seem all the more mysterious.*

Below *Besides carving huge statues, Easter islanders also made smaller objects such as these wooden figures.*

Recently archaeologists have tried to move the statues with tools used by the islanders. A few years ago one small statue was shifted a few yards. The figure was then levered upright in small stages by means of two long poles. Small stones were placed underneath the statue after each lift to keep it from tumbling back down. This demonstration was carried out with strong ropes, which would not have been available to the original builders. The experiment failed to show how the largest statues were moved.

Even greater mystery surrounds the identity of the people who erected the statues. It is thought that the first people arrived on Easter Island about AD400. Some six hundred years later, the first of the large statues was carved and erected. Work ceased about the time of the first European contact with the island.

The majority of statues on Easter Island lie abandoned in the quarry where they were originally built or on the mountain slopes.

According to the stories of the islanders, the statues were erected by a people called Long Ears. The Long Ears were the nobles of the island. They made their ears grow long by hanging heavy weights in them. The bulk of the population of the island were Short Ears. The Long Ears forced the Short Ears to work at building the statues.

The islanders say that eventually the Short Ears rebelled. In a frightful civil war, the Long Ears were killed. The Short Ears built no new statues and ignored those already existing.

Modern research has shown that the Short Ears who survive are Polynesians, similar to the inhabitants of other Pacific islands. However, the culture of the vanished Long Ears seems more similar to that of tribes in South America. It has been suggested that the Long Ears were a people driven into exile from South America. Others think that the Long Ears were Polynesians who developed their own culture without contact with South America.

Unfortunately, nobody is sure which of these ideas is correct. It is likely that we will never know, but one fact is certain. The statues will continue to stare out across Easter Island for many thousands of years to come.

Date Chart

About **AD400** The first people arrive on Easter Island.

About **1100** Large statues begin to be erected on the island.

About **1700** Civil war brings an end to the statue building.

1722 Admiral Roggeveen becomes the first European to land on the island.

Late 19th century Scientific investigation of the statues begins.

A straight line across the Nazcan Plain

The sun glares down from a cloudless sky. The air on the desert plain is becoming very hot and dry, but still the men toil on. The project they are working on has already taken many days. The priests say several days of hard work still lie ahead.

One of the priests places his pole upright on the ground, some distance from two others. Another priest gazes along the line formed by the three poles. He waves his hand to the left. The first priest moves slightly to the left. The priest, staring along the poles, holds his hand up in the air. He is satisfied that the three poles are in a straight line.

The men scramble forward. They throw small stones aside and roll larger rocks to one side. Slowly, step by step, the men reveal the underlying sand. This is of a different color from the loose stones. The men are creating a long, straight line across the desert floor. The priests supervise, making sure that the line stays completely straight.

This task is strenuous work, but the priests have declared that the lines are necessary, so the men work willingly.

The Plain of Nazca

In 1927, Toribio Mexta Xesspe was piloting his light aircraft over the Nazca Plain in Peru. He happened to glance downward and could hardly believe what he saw. Drawn across the surface of the desert were hundreds of lines and dozens of pictures. Xesspe could make out birds and spirals, together with long straight lines. As soon as he landed Xesspe reported his find.

In the years that followed, the markings on the Nazca Plain have been thoroughly investigated. Scientists now know how many lines and drawings exist on the Plain and how they were constructed. However, mystery still surrounds the question of why the lines were created.

For forty years, Maria Reiche, a German teacher, investigated the lines. She carefully mapped and recorded the markings. She found that more than 13,000 straight lines run across the Plain of Nazca, together with dozens of triangles, stars and spirals.

Left *A spiral design at Cantalloc, near Nazca, Peru, is typical of the patterns made by the Nazcans.*

The Mysterious Monkey

Of all the patterns and pictures drawn on the surface of the Nazca Plain, the most mysterious must be the gigantic monkey. Monkeys do not inhabit the area around Nazca, so nobody is sure how the people planning the figure knew about the existence of such creatures.

Perhaps most intriguing of all are the pictures that form part of the pattern. One of the most impressive is a stylized hummingbird, which has a wingspan of 60 meters (200 ft). Other animals of impressive size include a spider, a monkey and several birds.

Scientists know that the lines were formed by a very simple method. The sandy soil of the Nazca Plain is a pale yellow. On top of this sand lies a layer of black stones and pebbles. The lines were created by removing the black stones to reveal the light sand beneath.

Scattered beside the Nazca Plain are many pieces of broken pottery. Scientists have recognized this pottery as belonging to a culture that existed between the years 400BC and AD600. Designs on some of the pots resemble those on the Plain. The Nazca lines were constructed by the Indians of this culture.

The fingers of a giant lizard design cleared by Maria Reiche during her investigations of the lines.

The most mysterious feature of these pictures and lines is that they cannot be viewed from the ground. Seen by a visitor on foot, the lines appear to be jumbled furrows in the ground. It is only when seen from the air that the lines can be recognized as patterns and figures. Exactly why the Indians should want to mark out patterns they could not appreciate visually, nobody really knows. However, several suggestions have been made.

Some of the lines point toward important astronomical locations, such as the spot where the sun sets at the winter solstice. Maria Reiche believes that the Nazca lines were used to tell the time of year. Evidence against this idea is the fact that most lines point to nothing in particular and have no astronomical importance.

Above *One of the brightly painted pieces of pottery that are typical of Nazca culture.*

Right *This "spaceman" figure has led some people, such as Erich von Daniken, to believe that the lines were made for visiting beings from outer space.*

Left *The hummingbird figure with its beautiful design is the best known of all the Nazca lines.*

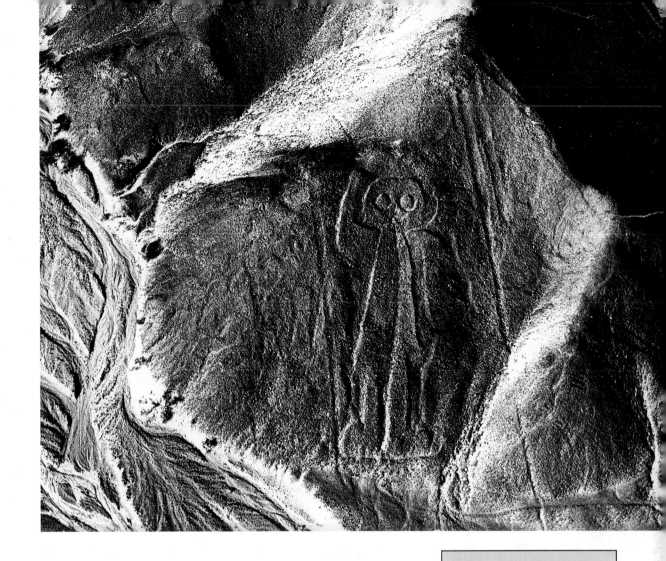

It is clear that the layout of the lines can only be seen from the air. The Swiss writer Erich von Daniken believes that the lines were built for the benefit of spacemen from another planet who visited Nazca centuries ago. However, few scientists agree with this idea.

Less controversial are the ideas of Jim Woodman, an American businessman. He believes that the ancient Nazcans were able to fly, using hot-air balloons, and therefore could see the beautiful designs from above. To prove his point, Woodman built a hot-air balloon using local materials. In November 1975, Woodman flew this balloon over the Nazca Plain.

However, despite the experiments of Jim Woodman, the research of Maria Reiche and many scientists, the mystery of the Nazca lines remains. Let us hope the research will continue until the complete story of this fascinating mystery is unraveled.

Date Chart

400BC The rise of the Nazca culture.

AD600 The collapse of the Nazca culture.

1927 The Nazca lines are rediscovered by Toribio Mexta Xesspe.

1945 Maria Reiche begins to study the Nazca lines.

1975 Jim Woodman flies over the Nazca Plain in a hot-air balloon.

Discovery of the mounds

Walter Pidgeon stares at the sight in front of him in wonder. Pidgeon has been led to this site by a local Indian man who promised to show him something unusual. Pidgeon moves forward and climbs to the top of the mound of earth. He looks around him. The mound seems to be the shape of an animal of some kind.

Pidgeon returns to the spot where the Indian waits for him. He takes out his notebook and asks the Indian some questions. It soon becomes clear that the Indian does not know very much about the strange mounds except that they were built a long time ago as a form of writing. Pidgeon eagerly writes down this information in his notebook.

Next Pidgeon sketches the outline of the mound in his book. Beyond this first mound, Pidgeon can see others scattered through the forest. He asks the Indian how many such mounds exist. He is told that there are several dozen to be found. Pidgeon realizes that he has stumbled upon a mystery from the past. He moves on toward the other mounds to examine them, excited and amazed by these strange forms.

The Mysterious Mounds

Scattered through the north-central states of Illinois, Wisconsin and Iowa and along the valleys of the Mississippi and Ohio rivers are some of the most mysterious constructions in the United States.

At these sites are found large mounds of earth. Some of the mounds are tall and impressive, others are low and easily missed. Many mounds are laid out in the shape of animals, while others have geometrical designs. In a forest in Iowa is a group of mounds representing ten bears, one bird and two straight lines.

The most famous of these artificial mounds is that known as the Great Serpent. It lies on a hill overlooking Brush Creek in Adams County, Ohio. The snake-shaped mound is 382 meters (1,253 ft) long, but barely three feet tall.

These mounds have been known for nearly two centuries; however, nobody is really certain why they were built. The first people to happen upon the mounds were European settlers who moved into the area during the early nineteenth century. They were greatly impressed by the size of the strange earth structures. It was clear that the American Indians then living in the area had not built them. The early Europeans thought that some mysterious civilization had once existed but had collapsed centuries earlier.

The Great Serpent Mound in Ohio is the most impressive of all the mounds in the area.

An Indian mound at Miamisburg, Ohio. Many other mounds have been destroyed or built over.

Below The Avondale Mounds in Mississippi as they appeared in the 1890s. A sight perhaps similar to that which Walter Pidgeon first saw.

In 1840 the historian Walter Pidgeon set out to survey the mounds. He measured and recorded many sites in the upper Mississippi Valley. Some of the mounds described by Pidgeon have since been destroyed by building projects or farming. Therefore his records are of great importance.

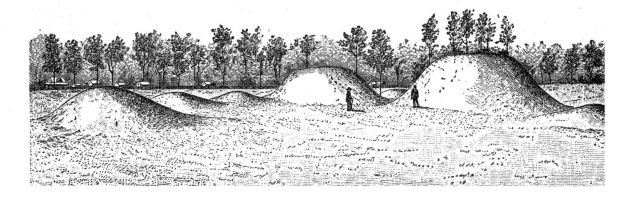

The Threatening Mounds

Many people visiting the mounds scattered across North America have experienced strange sensations. One of the most mysterious occurred when Robert Harner, a professor, visited the Great Serpent Mound in Ohio. He states that on a perfectly calm day, fallen leaves rose up into a column. At the same time Harner became aware of an "evil" force. As Harner fled, the feeling of evil left him and the leaves returned to the ground.

Above *A view of the many mounds to be found near Marietta, Ohio, in 1876.*

An Indian medicine man named De-coo-dah befriended Pidgeon and showed him the location of many mounds. De-coo-dah told Pidgeon that the ancestors of the Indians had built the mounds many years earlier as a form of writing. Unfortunately, Pidgeon could not persuade him to give him any more information.

Archaeologists have now been able to date the mounds. The first constructions began in about 1000 BC. These early constructions, which archaeologists have named Adena Mounds, were usually tombs. Some 800 years later, mound builders of the Hopewell culture began constructing the animal shapes from the earth. This phase lasted nearly 900 years. In the final period of mound building, known as the Mississippian, the Indians raised huge platforms of earth. Some of these were big enough to have formed the base for several large buildings.

Right *Some of the bowls and idols found in burial mounds in southern Missouri in the late nineteenth century.*

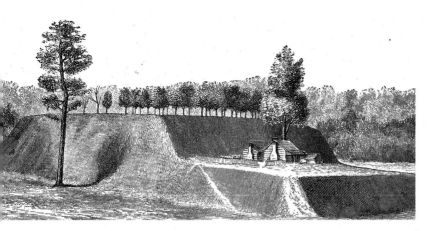

Mounds like this were used as the foundations for temples or burial sites.

When European explorers first came to the lower Mississippi Valley they found large mounds topped by wooden temples. They were told that the chief of the Indian tribe lived on one of the mounds.

Although scientists can be certain when the mounds were built and by whom, nobody knows why they were constructed. It seems that the later and larger mounds were burial places and the sites of temples. However, the purpose of the smaller mounds remains a mystery.

Some scientists believe that the mounds are representations of constellations of stars. Others think that the grassy banks may represent magical signs or be tribal totems. The only person who might have known the answer to the riddle was the medicine man De-coo-dah, but he is dead. The mounds remain just as mysterious as they were when they were first sited by Walter Pidgeon.

This engraving shows a mound used by the Indians as an idol for their religious ceremonies.

Date Chart

1000BC The Adena culture begins.

200BC The rise of the Hopewell culture.

AD600 The start of the Mississippian culture.

Early 19th century European settlers see the mounds of the upper Mississippi Valley.

1840 Historian Walter Pidgeon begins surveying the mounds.

1858 Walter Pidgeon publishes his book *Traditions of De-coo-Dah*, in which he describes the mounds he saw.

20th century Scientific research reveals the existence and dates of the Adena, Hopewell and Mississippian mound-building cultures.

Conclusion

Above *Heinrich Schliemann, the amateur archaeologist who discovered Troy, Mycenae and several other important Greek sites.*

Many mysteries that are both intriguing and puzzling have come to us from ancient times. The strange events and ruins of the past hint at forgotten secrets and excite the curiosity of the people who investigate them.

Many ancient mysteries remain unsolved due to a lack of information. The people who built Stonehenge and the mound builders of America could neither read nor write. This means that they were unable to record their ideas and the reasons for what they did. The Romans were literate, but no record of the fate of the IX Legion has survived.

Nobody is certain about the truth behind these mysteries, but many people have suggested theories. Some of these ideas sound sensible, others are strange and fanciful. It is possible that one or another of the theories may be the correct solution to each mystery. However, without more information the truth of a theory cannot be proved.

Right *Some ancient mysteries have been solved by archaeological excavations. The site of legendary Troy was discovered in Turkey in 1870.*

Above *Excavations today profit from the careful use of modern technology. Here archaeologists excavate Maiden Castle, England.*

Every year historians and archaeologists are learning more about the past. Fresh historical sites are explored and excavated. A famous example was the discovery of Troy in 1870. Ancient Greek legends and the Greek poet Homer, vividly described the city of Troy, but nobody was sure whether or not Troy had really existed. Then a German archaeologist, Heinrich Schliemann, set out to find the city. He followed the route suggested in Homer's poetry and began excavating an ancient town in Turkey. Before long Schliemann realized it matched exactly the ancient descriptions of Troy. His excavations proved that Troy had in fact existed and where it had stood.

In recent years, increasingly sophisticated equipment has been used by scientists investigating the past. It is possible that they may find new evidence concerning the ancient mysteries discussed in this book. Before long we may indeed know the solution to these tantalizing puzzles from the past.

Glossary

Ambushed   Taken by surprise by an enemy who has lain in wait to attack.

Archaeologists   Scientists who study the past by digging up ancient remains such as graves.

Architect   A person who designs buildings.

Brigantes   A tribe of Celts living in Britain at the time of the Roman invasion in AD43.

Celts   Certain groups such as the Britons and Gauls who inhabited much of Europe in Roman times.

Charnel houses   Buildings constructed to house dead bodies.

Civilization   The stage in the development of a people when they live together in an ordered community.

Constellations   Groups of stars.

Culture   The arts, tools, ideas and way of life of a certain people in a certain time.

Druids   The priests of the Celtic tribes.

Dynasty   A family whose members rule a country over a long period of time.

Excavate   To dig up an ancient site to discover what originally stood there.

Exorcists   Religious priests who drive away evil spirits through prayer.

Fortification   A structure built around a fortress or castle to give better protection from enemies.

Henge   A prehistoric monument consisting of a circular area enclosed by a bank and ditch.

Iceni   A tribe of Celts living in Britain at the time of the Roman invasion.

Legion   A division of Roman soldiers consisting of about 6,000 men.

Mummy   The body of an ancient Egyptian that has been preserved and wrapped in cloth.

Mummy case   A box, shaped like a human being and often richly decorated, that contained a mummy.

Pharaoh   The title given to the kings of ancient Egypt.

Polynesian   The inhabitants of a group of scattered islands in the Pacific Ocean, including Hawaii, Samoa, Tahiti, etc.

Prehistoric   A term used to describe a time before people could read or write. Stonehenge is a prehistoric monument.

Pyramid   A structure erected in ancient Egypt as a royal tomb. Pyramids have square bases and four sides that rise to a point.

Sacrifice   An offering, such as a valuable object or an animal, made to a god.

Sarcen   A kind of natural sandstone.

Solstice   The day of the year when the sun is farthest north of the equator or farthest south of the equator.

Standard   A flag or emblem used to show the central point of an army in battle.

Totem   An object, usually animal or plant, used by a group of people as their symbol or "mascot."

Further reading

If you would like to discover more about some of the ancient mysteries mentioned in this book, you might wish to read the following books:

The Blind Guards of Easter Island by Miriam W. Meyer. Raintree Publishers, 1977.
The Case of the Ancient Astronauts by I. J. Gallagher. Raintree Publishers, 1977.
The Mystery of Stonehenge by Nancy Lyon. Raintree Publishers, 1977.
People of Long Ago by Hendrick Willem Van Loon. Liveright, 1972.
Prisoner of the Mound Builders by Lloyd Harnisfeger. Lerner Publications, 1973.
Secret's of Tut's Tomb and the Pyramids by Stephanie A. Reiff. Raintree Publishers, 1977.
Unsolved Mysteries of Time and Place and Space by Griffith Jones. EMC Publishing, 1980.

Picture Acknowledgments

The publishers would like to thank the following for providing the pictures in this book:
Geoscience Features 23, 25 (top); The Hutchison Library 11; Photri 41 (top); Ronald Sheridan's Picture Library 44 (top left), 44 (bottom) 45; South American Pictures 34 (bottom left), 35, 36 (bottom), 37; Topham 6, 12 (bottom), 17, 24, 25 (left), 30 (bottom); Western Americana 40, 41 (bottom), 42 (top), 42 (bottom), 43 (top), 43 (bottom); Zefa 7, 10, 12 (top), 13, 16, 18, 19, 29, 30 (top), 31.

Index